Also by Jill Bialosky

POETRY

*The Players*
*The Skiers: Selected Poems*
*Intruder*
*Subterranean*
*The End of Desire*

FICTION

*The Prize*
*The Life Room*
*House Under Snow*

PROSE

*Poetry Will Save Your Life: A Memoir*
*History of a Suicide: My Sister's Unfinished Life*

ANTHOLOGY

*Wanting a Child* (edited with Helen Schulman)

# ASYLUM

# ASYLUM

*A Personal, Historical, Natural Inquiry in 103 Lyric Sections*

## JILL BIALOSKY

*Alfred A. Knopf*
*New York*
*2020*

Grateful acknowledgment is made to Farrar, Straus and Giroux and The Orion
Publishing Group for permission to reprint excerpts from Cantos I, II, III,
IV, V, XIII, XXXIV from The Inferno of Dante: A New Verse Translation by
Robert Pinsky. Translation copyright © 1994 by Robert Pinsky. Reprinted by
permission of Farrar, Straus and Giroux and The Orion Publishing Group.

Library of Congress Cataloging-in-Publication Data
Names: Bialosky, Jill, author.
Title: Asylum : a personal, historical, natural inquiry in 103 lyric
sections / Jill Bialosky.
Description: First edition. | New York : Alfred A. Knopf, 2020.
Identifiers: LCCN 2019043146 (print) | LCCN 2019043147 (ebook) |
ISBN 9780525657095 (hardcover) | ISBN 9780525657101 (ebook)
Subjects: LCSH: Grief—Poetry | LCGFT: Poetry.
Classification: LCC PS3552.I19 A94 2020 (print) | LCC
PS3552.I19 (ebook) | DDC 811/.54—dc23
LC record available at https://lccn.loc.gov/2019043146
LC ebook record available at https://lccn.loc.gov/2019043147

Frontispiece by Dana Montlack
Jacket image: Original illustration by Mary S. Morse
Jacket design by John Gall

For she who once saw the stars

Reachable, near and not lost, there remained in the midst
of the losses this one thing: language. It, the language,
remained, not lost, yes in spite of everything.

—PAUL CELAN


Look around:
See how things all come alive—
By death! Alive!

—PAUL CELAN

# CONTENTS

PART II.

PART III.

# PART IV.

# PART V.

# A S Y L U M

# PRELUDE

It was like the music of an afflicted bird,
a screech owl from the underworld, querulous,
seductive, a fugue of death. Or so you thought—
taunting its refrain, one sound imitating the other,
as if it had entered your spirit & was your own voice.
It took years, maybe decades, before you realized
you had gotten it wrong: it was the fugue of life.

# PART I.

*Love which in gentle hearts is quickly born*

I.

There she is, the woman who once inhabited
these rooms, drank tea from this cup,
her shape in the cushion, isn't that hers?
Those shelves filled with books from the bookshops
of her youth—Rilke, Plath, Akhmatova, Stevens, Strand,
afternoons spent in worn leather chairs
beneath the dim yellow lamplight by the window,
slow-motion of curling leaves heralding a fallen season.

II.

Even the rats will not emerge in the whiteout—
they sometimes come out
before dusk reminding us of our fear
of creatures we can't see
when we venture to Riverside Park—
its rocky precipices, beat-up lawns, groves of elm—
at the edge of the Hudson to watch the tugboats
& remind ourselves we live on an island of buildings.
The mayor warned us not to go out.

III.

It was snowing in St. Petersburg, spoors from the tall
poplar trees floated like pigeon feathers in the air,
June or July, I barely remember,
everything foreign, faces of the passersby
hardened by history, American labels at odds
in the shop windows, the day we climbed
the winding stairs where Dostoevsky's hero,
Raskolnikov ascended to commit murder & afterwards
looked down the iron staircase to contemplate his fate.
I was in a mood where the text was the city,
furloughed from my country, no longer mother to my son,
wife to my husband, in my dreams always the same age.
Everywhere the façade of buildings,
lure of the canals, crumbling palaces.

IV.

Together we circled
the rings, a boy, he was still learning
& we moved slowly,
picking up rhythm as we traveled,
we would see it all, digging our blades
to find traction, balance, to free the mind
of doubt, falling,
occasionally bumping up
against the outer edge—
it would take years if we were lucky—
stumbling in the face of reason,
*O muses, O geniuses of art,*
*O memory,* our blades crushing
the ice.

V.

of the childless mother,
of an unanswered text,

of the silent corridors
in the home for the aged—*there is no loneliness like theirs,*

of the patter of rain,
of the hollow sound of a violin, of listening to Sir Neville Marriner

perform at the Academy of St. Martin in the Fields, the music flowing
from a pair of speakers that are deaf to all outside them,

of the frigid, of the unfriended,
of the single digits, the dishwasher cycle,

of a summerhouse boarded for the season,
of a foreign language, of marriage, of motherhood,

of addiction, of failure to be heard or understood,
of birds hiding in the sarcophagus of a bereaved tree.

## VI.

After the wind tore up
our backyard & in the morning pollen
soaked the grass, forsythia burst forth,
loose twigs hurled into the gutters,
arthritic branches in the drive,
is it the chaos of God's will,
we wondered. One had no faith.
Another fickle. One a believer.
Another dreamy & skittish.
Minors, we collected stones,
fished for worms in the ground,
picked leaves, traced the veins,
as we tracked them in our palms,
plucked poison berries, buried
dead birds. We did not know
of war or murder or the difference of skin.
We knew only that from which we were.

## VII.

Each season with its privileges.
Fat turkeys strutting their wings,
families of deer, mutations of bugs,
worms in the garden, ants drunk
on the sweet sap of peonies (they crawl
in & open the petals) & beyond the horses
trapped in their asylum, nudging their long
noses into troughs, in winter
backs saddled with navy blankets.
& all day the sighing, whether wind
or horses, or an ailing deer.

VIII.

We can't see anything but ice
crusting at the moldings

& the white fury
of inevitable, unstoppable snow.

Not
streetlamps & reflections

of light. Nor parked cars

on the side of the road,
now tiny mountains. Shrouds.

Nor the cloud of our breath.
Everything eviscerated

by snow's bleak & debilitating
camouflage, so that blind,

or unwilling,

we could not see. It was like
the last day

of the end of an era, it was like,

no, it was like nothing
we'd ever seen.

IX.

& in the mornings sometimes awoke so cold
—the wind in Iowa City was brutal—
those days of doubt, those days of troubled land,
that I did not want to get out of bed &
creep down crooked stairs to the bathroom
on the second floor shared with two other graduate students,
one also a poet who was innocuously quiet & thin,
& the other a medical student studying the art of the body.
I ate the same avocado, tomato & cream cheese
sandwich for lunch & dinner—later
in New York City it was pasta shells
with marinara or olive oil & broccoli—
I liked the order & monotony, because to want
was to tempt the gods, because modesty
was the equivalent of survival.

X.

We were told there were things hidden from us,
*there had to be more,* powers & forces we were not aware of,
& could not understand but that we must surrender our trust,
the flap of a butterfly wing, for instance, could change the balance
of the universe.

XI.

In Iowa City, the restaurant
where I worked on the weekend
for extra cash, I befriended
another waitress, blond & blue-eyed,
she grew up in one of the remote farms outside of town
where wind was ruthless & could overturn a truck.
I was the first Jew she'd ever met.
I caught her watching me sometimes.

XII.

Why I thought I needed to rent a third-floor attic,
why I thought one mattress on the floor, a desk, a vanity
with a mirror—why whether from grief, abundance,
freckled blue-black sky, soundless rain, humanity's pain,
endless desire, the poem came—

XIII.

Once a bird flew in, its wings
soaring into the stained-glass arch
of the ceiling & like a fallen angel, fell to the ground.
Reciting passages from the book
of agony, of remorse, of childhood, elegy & song,
we did not know what was real & what was allegory,
what we believed, those days we looked into the eye
of God (the light above the arc was said to be everlasting)
& prayed for our names to be entered—
those who will live & those destined
to the world to come.

XIV.

Faith turned on the milkman who delivered
our milk, the mailman who brought the mail

& slipped it in the metal slot. We could hear it fall
down the hollow tunnel. The repairmen

who came to fix what was broken. It was the house
where I grew up. I knew every alcove, chipped tile,

swoosh of air when we opened the laundry chute
& peered into its envelope of darkness,

the way light fell through the living room window,
exposing the cracks & later slept behind the tree

in the back, every hiding place.

XV.

Because she believed (she was like this)
that there had to be more, because the father
of her children was taken from her, her Orpheus—
as if struck down by a cruel god, because
once the patriarch died, it was as if
we were cast off like seeds of the misbegotten,
our mother demanded we all get in the car
& we trolled the neighborhood. She preferred
to surrender to a lawn of crocuses, a field of daylilies,
bearded iris & foliage of complicit tulips.
*I told you,* she would say.

XVI.

From my window on the third floor
I could see every now & then
a car creep down Bowery Street,
a girl on the sidewalk jumping rope, a mother
holding the hands of her children, a woman
thrusting her nose into the burst
of a sunflower as if into the face
of God. Land flat & houses simple
& architecturally inelegant. I found little
beauty in the scatter of maples
that lined the blocks except that yes,
the braided trees held
the little that was.

XVII.

I knew by then
that anything was possible—
once we witnessed a child's cheek nearly cut out
from another skater's blade during a fall—
as he swerved in & out of the skaters,
the triple axel of *envy, gluttony, & pride*
*igniting their hearts,* always someone
who wanted to outdo another,
we had to witness all of it,
because it had already happened,
I had to be vigilant, cautious. Sometimes
I held his hand tight.
Because I knew.

XVIII.

Like a flock of dispossessed
in a city of converts, we found our way
to the Shamrock where the bikers
congregated to play pool.
To give of our body & to touch another's body
felt like a religious act, like an act
of loyalty & trust, not necessarily
lust but lust of the dispossessed,
lust of the insatiable,
of the lonely, lust of the powerful
& privileged, lust of harm, of longing,
lust that desecrates the soul
& the body, terrible & never-ending,
lust that one sees in the eyes
of another,
lust of the violent,
lust of the dominant,
of the depraved,
lust that sees a body
as simply a vessel
for one's lust.

XIX.

Some cultures believed if you stood tall with your back against a tree, because they were steady, in sync with the circadian & seasonal rhythm of the universe & breathed your longing into its ballast, if you were patient & focused, your beloved would find you.

XX.

If someone was kind enough to take us driving out to the long roads
that veered away from cornfields to the farms, pig roasts & parties

that lasted until dawn, where on occasion we found ourselves
in bed with someone we hardly knew & awoke laughing to escape

the shame & thrill of it, then for that time there was a brief sojourn
from the asylum in which the poem was held prisoner, asylum for which

there was a cell that carried our self-doubts, a cell for lack
of confidence, a cell for fear, for rage, a cell for emptiness, a cell

for want, a cell for which there is no name for, as there is no name
for the ways we hoped language would save us.

XXI.

Beneath a canopy
of wild vines & flowers to signify

before our witnesses, the home we'd make,
because we must be accountable, true,

we said our blessings, *I belong to you*
*& you belong to me,* it was before

fear & joy collided, before the wind
screamed & the world divided, it was before

time, before we knew, it was another
era. It was when we believed if we toiled,

if we suffered, if we were citizens
of the sublime, scrupulous,

divine, we would be redeemed,
it was before pity, no it was something else,

it was before we believed.

XXII.

Those long afternoons we trudged
through the North Woods.
Some days it was insufferable,
the cold & still we traveled through
the abyss where the Black Cherry, Pin Oak,
& Red Maple were stripped of their clothes
& the wind slapped our faces, furies
blotting our eyes, no foreseeable
path in the snow & still we made the journey.
Sometimes we stumbled upon more
than we wanted (how to explain a body
with a blanket over a subway grate for warmth,
or the babble of the mind's asylum, those decorated
with gold of the privileged, those without shoes). Still
it was like an accident of joy, like a chorus gathering,
like a gift from a mysterious god,
it was like the unknown whisper of trees in the park's
forest. It was the shadow
life I feared.

XXIII.

Washing dishes, occasionally looking out at the wood
& at one bird circling the nest & at the pollen dust
raining from the greenery that has gathered,
not simply as a nuisance in our pool, but as a miracle
of procreation, & it was as if seeing
pollen for the first time.

XXIV.

& so we looked for patterns, for order to ward off chaos. For aberrations that might offer a hint. Because we were seekers, because grief had transformed us.

XXV.

Trees breathe in oxygen and breathe out carbon dioxide, releasing energy
& water into the air. Some birth flowers of only one sex & others both
male & female flowers, the same way we bear fruit to those we bear &
those who bear us. Even trees are in the presence of the divine, we were
told. In some cultures, they are thought to have a consciousness, to feel
happiness & pain. Some are twisted, some antithetical to the profane.

XXVI.

We wanted him
to know that a tree
was a living being.
We wanted him
to know it was precious.
It was before
the frost. The leaves
had turned all colors
of fire. The maples stood tall
their branches linked
like a proud family.
We drilled into the trunk to tap
the maple & free
the blood of the tree,
its sweetness, its
thin drooling sap.

XXVII.

Pollen, like sperm to humans & animals, the male reproductive
vehicle which fertilizes the egg of the female ovary of the same species
instrumental in the continued life cycle of plants & trees.
It is a "powdery cloud of fine yellowish grains, each tiny grain a single cell
enclosed in a protective coating." If the pollen can't move about
in search of a mate, wind, bees, birds, bats, butterflies
will carry pollen to its female source.

XXVIII.

In tree pose, otherwise known as Vriksasana, our Yoga teacher says to
stand on one leg for balance. Move the sole of the other foot into the inner
thigh of the standing leg. Once you've found your balance put your hands
in prayer in front of your chest & then raise them over your head, arms
to ears, stand tall, steady, grow, she says, root yourself to the ground.
Breathe.

XXIX.

Under microscope, magnifying glass,
using magnets & electricity, pin & tuning fork,
lumbar punctured, photographed, sketched,
hypnotized, documented, compared, analyzed,
tortured, starved, etherized, objectified
& concretized, held prisoner
by the perpetrators of a science—
by the history of an era, by the myth
of the unsolvable math of the mercurial mind.

XXX.

We kept our heads down.
We were entranced. Focused.
Sometimes we could not see
anything before us. That's what it
required. One year I had forgotten
the first leaves of spring. I had forgotten
all the years of toil. I looked up &
trees had flowered. All it took
was waiting out the bleak winter.
The *hemisphere of darkness*. The color
was lime green. I wanted to tell her—
*This is what it's like.*

XXXI.

Should sleep come,
*Don't Let Me Be Lonely*—
considers the poet,
& her inability to sleep—
if on televisions
breaking news flashes,
civilians struck down by a terrorist's truck,
or one magazine's worth of madness,
& continuously along the bottom of our screen,
a number for a suicide hotline.

# PART II.

*Beware how you come in and whom you trust*

XXXII.

Like just awaking
drenched, they persist,
ghosts in our poems,
ghosts in our imagination,
ghosts in our waking hours, ghosts
who elude philosophers, poets,
scientists, psychiatrists,
therapists & doctors, ghosts
who perpetuate,
who guileless,
will not keep quiet,
who preside over the populace,
& unknowingly rob
the living, ghosts
who *made their own house
their gallows,* Dante says,
will never rest.

## XXXIII.

*Suicide isn't an issue that can simply be . . . It never will . . . are affected by each act . . . who grieve . . .* Ms. Bialosky, author of History of *. . . lost her youngest sister, Kim, twenty-six years ago to carbon monoxide poisoning in the garage . . . forever altered the way in which . . . "the world around me" . . . says that her sister's suicide would creep into . . . and frighten her . . . such an act will always remain . . . up to the ones left behind to . . . yet the hauntings . . . could be prevented in the first place.*

XXXIV.

*Carbon monoxide is a dangerous gas that is colorless, odorless and tasteless. The gas does not survive for long in the atmosphere and breaks down to form a part of ground-level ozone. Carbon monoxide can affect any vertebrate living being and is highly toxic. If inhaled, carbon monoxide combines with hemoglobin (which carries the oxygen from the lungs and carbon dioxide to the lungs) and makes it ineffective to do its normal function. The inhalation of carbon monoxide results in the formation of carboxyhemoglobin, which reduces the flow of oxygen to the body parts and causes severe seizure, and eventually death can occur.*

XXXV.

Every April a requiem, a re-awaking of dawn, the same chorus
& players. The garage door sealed, gas turned on & the girl,

once addled by a broken heart, by a mind that won't stop,
by the tickertape of loneliness, there she is again, slumped

against the door, hair tangled around her neck, effervescent
eyes closed, rings & bracelets catching the hint of morning sun,

the myth of the girl unraveling, when the boy who arrives
to cut the lawn, opens the garage door to fetch the lawnmower

& finds her. The birds are trumpets & flutes, the wind a piano.
Daffodils are frozen. Shock of forsythia withering in the cold,

tulips trampled. Pollen has not yet released, buds not yet opened.
It is April again & all the trees bow for the final coda.

XXXVI.

A summer in which my mother's mind
begins to dissolve. In which grief
& suffering calcified her brain cells,
losing portions of thought, retaining
only threads of perception. Another
summer in which we had to pack up
the house of my childhood, the house
in which at thirteen I rocked
our July baby & pressed my lips to the warm
hairless top of her head, careful of the fontanel,
the soft spot that had not yet healed. A summer
when perpetrators toppled headstones
in the Jewish cemetery.

XXXVII.

Marriage of trees,
Marriage of birdcalls,
Marriage of thought & action,
of mother & child,
of youth & abandon,
Marriage of black & white
& yellow & brown,
Marriage of lust & pleasure,
Pleasure & lust,
Hiding & revealing,
Reason & unreason,
Abeyance & succession,
Seeker & sought,
Belief & disbelief,
Preservation &
Destruction,
Marriage of heaven
& hell.

## XXXVIII.

Because her mother was sleeping the sleep of the quiescent,
because her boyfriend did not listen to the words of her torment,

because her sister was in New York practicing, which is a form of writing,
carefully selecting words & then erasing them, phrase upon phrase,

hiding & revealing, rhyme & half-rhyme, enjambment & syllabics,
form & meaning, narrative & lyric, thought & substance,

because the night was unbearable & would never end,
because she was yet to become the woman who fought the girl inside her,

because the girl's thought, long enough to scribble a note, long enough
to turn the key in a car, met action & now she is gone.

XXXIX.

Daffodils, survivors, of *the cruellest month*
*tossing their heads in sprightly dance* from the ground arise—

beautiful long spines & yellow crowns—
Tulips, Plath's flower (Hughes fancied a fox),

*too excitable . . . too red.* What we thought would thrive
we found a family of fragile evergreens

we had planted one year—bottom needles eaten out
by starving deer, one we had to tie to a stake—

to keep steady & alive.

XL.

When he was small,
I rented a little studio
in a building on Ninety-fifth Street so I could have a room
of my own to write. The studio was the size of a bathroom.
It was dirty & dark with grey painted floors
& a shared bathroom in the hallway.
I never met another inhabitant, though if I ventured to the bathroom
I occasionally saw a sliver of light underneath one of the closed doors.
The only window in the studio faced the fire escape
where pigeons liked to coo & I found that once
I was in my studio, no words came.
Every month I signed the rent check for the studio we could not afford
hoping that I would find an hour's peace in that space
in which to "arrange my thoughts," that might then correspond
to a line of verse, or a paragraph of prose.
I don't know why I needed to rent a studio
in which to encourage words that fought
against my desire to claim them.

The boy who arrived
to cut the grass
smelled gasoline
& opened the garage door.
The police officer
the boy called after
he found her slumped
inside the car,
broke inside the house
to find her mother asleep
without the knowledge
that her life as she knew it
was already forever altered.
The mother whose loss is unrecoverable.
The two friends she partied with that night—one of which
knew her since preschool at Montessori,
their mothers (mine & hers) became close friends.
There is *that* mother.
The sister in New York, the sister in California,
the sister who is three months pregnant,
the father no one knows how to find,
the estranged stepbrother & sister,
the great-aunt who loved her like a granddaughter,
whose walls hold her finger paintings,
teachers, classmates, principals,
therapist whose card was found in her wallet,
the boy for whom she thought was worth her life . . .
The high school girl writing a paper on *History of a Suicide*.

## XLII.

like the snap of a branch,
like the terror of the wind,
like roots dug up,
like worms in their undergrowth,
like the rat on the pavement
smashed by the wheels of a car
into an inconceivable pancake,
like the inexplicable act
of making a noose
hanging it from the ceiling
& tightening it around the neck,
like the argument in a forest,
like a person who knows things,
a person who can't forget
a person who probes,
persists & is unkind,
like the mind hating itself,
like the wind giving in to logic,
like thought murdering the body,
like the night when the resilience
of lavender, woody, spiky,
tucked in the corner
where deck meets earth,
gave up & failed to thrive.

XLIII.

Because it was Christmas & I was home
with my fiancé, her blue eyes bright

burned with the brightness of knowing & barely
a fleck of gloom, because she was young

& brave & still wore cheap & sexy dresses
in which only she made elegant & though

she sometimes came home intoxicated,
& vomited from drink & wept alone

suffering from the human syndrome of need,
want & abandon, she still slept wearing

a Bugs Bunny sweatshirt, made us all scrambled
eggs, nursed her beloved cat, gossiped with girl-

friends on her phone & slept stone-cold
into the morning like Sleeping Beauty

awaiting a kiss, in a room under a vaulted
ceiling of a synagogue of the holy

& depraved, where I too once slept
in the cradle of despair & rage.

# XLIV.

Turquoise plates extremely rare, as the orange footed
Fiesta bowl that decorated our table & held the sour

green apples she adored, books, clothes, bronze baby shoes,
portraits & paintings, images & memories alive through objects

stripped from the house in which they once resided & all
but a few precious items sold to a liquidator. I remember her glee,

a hero for what no mother should bear, more permanent
than any object, at the flea markets in Chardon

where we trolled for treasured pieces of Fiestaware.
Once we found her favorite, though she did not like to choose—

(*which one died,* she said, confused, pointing to the photos
of her four daughters above her bed once she moved

into the care home's prelude for the soon-to-be-dead)—a vintage ivory
pitcher that now most likely resides in a stranger's abode.

# PART III.

*Now we descend into the sightless zone.*

XLV.

Because the Nile River ran red with blood,
livestock diseased, locusts, boils, hailstorms, three days of darkness,

every firstborn threatened by an avenging angel—you had to mark
the door with blood of a sacrificed lamb so that God would pass over it.

Because to identify those when deported to the camps in Nazi-occupied
Eastern Europe they were required to sew a yellow Jewish Star

on their jacket. Later, in the camps, a white armband
with a blue Jewish Star bound on their left arm. Babies in prams, too

had to wear them, infants tossed in the air and used as targets
for the machine guns. Oh, holy war. Because someone painted a Swastika

on the door of a dorm room where three Jewish students reside,
*Jews will not replace us,* because in the complex, only the apartments

of minorities had signs marking their doors. Because on a college
campus, a Swastika was carved into the purity of white fallen snow.

XLVI.

Because gods are threatening to tear down branches,
uproot trees, because there is no réprimande, recourse,

no release, rain unleashes in downpours, wind casting
for answers, for crimes committed, souls humiliated, denied

passage, denied rest, there is no end to the flooding, no end
of grief. In downpours, rain is unleashed.

XLVII.

Friends take turns,
it's been over a year now,
around-the-clock vigil,
O cries, laments, shrieks
the impossibility
of such a crime realized,
*heaven expel him, he is not wanted here,*
taken as he did, a mother's firstborn son,
riding his bicycle along the river,
groceries for his mother in his basket,
one of eight victims randomly
struck down by a terrorist's
truck—spilled along the graveled
path, a stream of milk & blood.

XLVIII.

*What I saw were naked women who did not look like women anymore*
*shoved in boxcars—no light inside—transporting them like cattle to*
*Auschwitz, no hair, no pubic hair, some committed suicide with the silver*
*wires in the car . . .*

## XLIX.

Another spray of violence,
boys shot dead for the color
of skin or for the "supremacy"
of a "race"; a man choked by the police
for selling single cigarettes (*I can't breathe, I can't breathe*),
schoolchildren taken down by a lone terrorist,
eldest members of the Tree of Life synagogue, massacred,
souls who live inside those that mourn they can never kill,
they, the purveyors of hate, I told him, my cherished one,
while in another room of the synagogue, a bris,
a ceremony to celebrate the birth of a baby boy
to seal his covenant is taking place.

L.

What are words when they meet the action
of what they attempt to modify?
What is snow, but series on series of crystals of ice.
What is pollen, but a golden granular element of microscopic grains
released from the male part of a flower.
What are weeds, but the aftermath of seeds the wind blows
into a yard & threaten to overtake.
What is grass, but a blade of energy & a single instance of a mass.

**LI.**

*Fire is 1/60 of hell, honey is 1/60 of the manna, Shabbat is 1/60
of the World to Come, sleep is 1/60 of death, & dreams 1/60 of prophecy.*

LII.

Pollen is everywhere.
Blossoms are at the very edge
of becoming & there is no more winter
(global warming is destroying our idea of what we've come to know),
except for the winters of our memory, winters where the girl
in the blue snowsuit (a sister) tasted snow for the first time.
There is no more winter except for the winters
of our memory. Winters where we mourned,
trapped in the mind's circling inferno & could not get out,
winter where the boy surpassed the age in which his mother's sister,
forever young, departed.

LIII.

*Pretty, pretty robin!*
*Under leaves so green*
*A happy blossom*
*Hears you sobbing, sobbing,*
*Pretty, pretty robin*

LIV.

Hustling her new book on NPR, a marriage counselor
says most marriages survive out of kindness.

Romanticism has been a detriment to us, a philosopher cants.
*The reason motherhood was largely excised from poetry*

*before the 1960s is because poets feared exposing truth*
*to their offspring, or sentimentalizing their art, says the poet on podcast.*

At lunch with a writer I admire I listen to her describe
her experience. *My editor did not understand it, so I had to frame*

*it for her & my words became my book. What about the daily*
*care of children, how does this enter the poem, the poet insists.*

*The words became my book.*

LV.

Snow of childhood,
of dreams, of our poems
& discontent, snow of our memories,
some distorted,
forgotten, trod upon, rendered
to a whiteout, snow that dusts
bridges, highways, roofs,
that tastes of rust
& weighs on the branches,
*O don't forget them,*
insufferable snow that falls
on the pots that hold
the pods of the dead
in the brilliance
of the outdoor gazebo
we see from the window
of the care home for the aged,
to praise our matriarch,
our boots wet, snow in our hair,
look how pale she is, look
what she has bore, those veins
in which flowed the blood
that flowed into us—

LVI.

In Yoga class the teacher says
Utkatasana, or awkward pose, chair pose,
comes from the ancient stance of two warriors
in opposition. In this pose, we place
our standing feet together, our chest out
& our arms stretched by our ears
& squat without losing alignment in our back.
*Utkatasana* comes from the Sanskrit *utkata,*
which means "fierce, proud, high, haughty, superior,
immense, large, difficult." It is a warrior pose.
You must breathe through your struggle,
she says. Set your intention. Breathe.

PART IV.

*If you remove*
*a little branch from any one of these pieces*
*Of foliage around us, the thoughts you have*
*Will also be broken off.*

LVII.

To avoid the perils
of poison ivy & ticks, we put on sweatpants, long-sleeve shirts & waders.
Sometimes on our treks, we'd find empty liquor bottles,
ashes from a woodpile. Snakes in the grasses. Dead mice.
Sometimes we carried long sheaths to make our way
through the bramble. We were in Dante's woods
of suicides transformed into gnarled trees,
souls bound up in knots, where harpies
feed on these who cannot grieve,
where some had lost their way. *What if, what if,* the birds chirped,
*it could happen again, all of it* & so we kept going,
fighting our betrayers, battling those who engaged
in violence, pursued bestial appetites, those without faith
& moral guidance, those who deprive themselves of the world—
warriors of survival, swatting away blizzards of flies, nettle
that nicked at our heels & left scratches, wasps that stung, ticks
carrying disease in the undergrowth. We waded in the asylum,
where some have fallen & others ravaged,
scorched from sun, crowded out or decimated
by animals, insects, vines, some with nubs & scabs,
wounded & shriveled. We trudged through the undergrowth,
trembling beneath ancient layers of broken twigs, dead leaves,
decomposed insects, animal bones, who knew what else,
where myths deem hell beneath the ground.

LVIII.

I don't know if I was still in dream
when I awoke & heard the faint sound, it was like someone moaning.
I kept hearing it again & again, still coming awake, through the pane
in the window. Later I discovered wasps had made a nest
in the crack of wood outside underneath the frame—
their nests made of paper—where I sleep.
It was the hum of the brush of the wing creating a vibration
in the wind (what a lot of effort living). Sometimes when they loom
over a flower they catch pollen in their wings
& bring it back to their larvae.

LIX.

A pigeon flew overhead
& kept circling our table
at an outdoor café—
a year had passed, soon
we would lay the headstone,
what did it want,
(desperate as we still were
to assign meaning)
fluttering its filthy wings,
circling & fluttering,
fluttering & circling,
a scavenger in a city
of scavengers,
*she thought she could fool*
*infinity?* It was pitiful,
no food, or crumbs,
nothing the pigeon
could have wanted only
our blood-red wine & napkins
folded in our laps—
we were among the living—
there was no entrance back.

LX.

Once we name it, does it cease to matter?

LXI.

Metamorphized into trees
that for eternity bleed
if cut or pruned or preyed
upon, forever cast into hell's
seventh circle *the lip above*
*the chasm of pain which holds the din*
*of infinite grief,* unable to settle
neither in heaven, nor the underworld
the self-slaughtered.
Hinduism considered it "soul murder,"
Muslims, hellfire & in the eternal life
forever to inflict themselves with pain.
Aristotle considered self-murder
a crime against one's self & country, Jews denied
a proper burial. *And for your lifeblood*
*I will require a reckoning.*
There is no logic to divine,
no pleasure or pain greater
than human stain.

LXII.

What if it is those who survive who never rest?

LXIII.

The wife of a friend
of my husband's,
under the delirium
of a pill to fall asleep,
because sleep
would not come, awoke
to their apartment on fire,
flames around the baby's
crib like the burning sand
& fiery rain, the hell
of burning flesh
their baby suffered,
& never again
did this family
return to the apartment—
nor the city in which
fire blazed—

LXIV.

This family did not return to the city in which the fire started.
This family did not return to be this family the same way in which
another family (the poet's) did not return to be the same family
once the garage sealed shut, the car turned on & the girl slept forever.

LXV.

Because the only way
to make it quiet
was to sleep,
because longing had led
to no reasonable transformation,
because to want was to fail,
to blame was to incite anger,
because to live with pain
meant entering a vortex
of weeping.
Because her body hurt,
because, hopeless, she did not know
that it would pass, because
she was slowly dying
like an annual flower,
never to come back,
because there was unattended
trauma, loss, an unexpected
frost, a sleepless endless mantra,
a decomposing, an unimaginable
future, because she did not know
the wreckage her leaving cost
& all the life she had before her.

LXVI.

An iPhone buzzes,
a text or an email,
a correspondence,

question, réquisition,
someone checking in, lost,

or in need
of an answer. Voices
of the known

& the unknown, streaming
on Facebook, Instagram, Twitter,
a running

stream of voices
residing in infinity's cloud.

LXVII.

In basements, backseats of cars,
hidden stairwells, boys made out with & suffered
(some a waste of time), free clinics signed in
to collect methods, bathrooms held hostage
cutting temple, math, weed smoked, counters
cleared, *pocketing tips, saving coins*
libraries entered, English papers painstakingly composed,
friends loved & forsaken, mistakes & humiliations
& victories, all of it stored in the mind's
encyclopedia rewritten in the form of obscure
& sometimes haunted dreams.

LXVIII.

I was washing dishes in the sink.
My hands were wet. The baby was crying.

I was past due on my deployments.
Listening to the radio I heard the poet's voice,

her fear of being deemed a domestic poet—
(you will not undo us the patriarch said)

& the disdain in which it is held—
& all the while the baby cried

& still there were the towels spinning
in the dryer that needed folding,

bottles to wash, formula to mix
& warm & the oven in which another poet

rested her head that needed my attention.

LXIX.

We can see the window she peered out
in The Fountain House in the center of St. Petersburg
on the second floor flat of the Sheremetevsky Palace
(*God preserves everything*) where in exile Akhmatova
wrote her poems. In the garden notes
to her memory are bound to the trunk of a tree by a ribbon
of packaging tape. It was the White Nights
where the sun sank at dawn—and night never ended,
nothing linear, orderly or free of chaos except
for the bitter sweetness of espresso we sipped in the garden
where flowers must have grown so very long ago
under the tree of bondage.

LXX.

Listening to Symphony Hall
on Sirius radio, to the "Pines of Rome,"
& Hayden's Symphony No. 22 in E flat major,
known as "The Philosopher,"
followed by "Artist's Life" by Johann Strauss II
(Strauss learned to play the violin in secret,
because, so as not to suffer the artist's life,
his father wished him to be a banker) composed
after Austria's defeat in battle, the melody
meant to infuse breath into bleakness, elegy into declaration,
creation into harmony, even in a time of ravage & war.

LXXI.

One winter, years later, after the transmission blew
the mechanic discovered the skeleton of a dead animal,

(he took a photo on his iPhone, that I cannot unsee)
a raccoon or cat that had crawled in to protect itself

from the freeze in the hood of the car we drove to the beach,
& sometimes left for weeks deserted on the drive,

sometimes for a season, gathering pollen in spring,
drift of fallen leaves, snow in winter, endless rain,

& must have tried in vain—sometimes mice in the hood
were hungry enough to eat the wires—

to get out but could not find a way.

# PART V.

*To get back up to the shining world from there*
*My guide and I went into that hidden tunnel*

LXXII.

The monarchs are born. They are smaller this year.
One is feasting on the zinnias in my pot on the deck.
Its wings open & close as if sucking in the nectar.
We chased monarchs when my son was small.
Once we caught one, we watched it flutter in the net
(so fragile we could have crushed it)
& flung it back into the wild too beautiful—
with its tapestry of black & orange, regal,
named after the Prince of Orange in Holland—
to prison in a jar.

LXXIII.

Butterflies sometimes mate as soon as the male emerges
from its pupa and will help the female to shed hers,
undressing her by pulling off her silk coat.
Others mate when the male courts the female in the air,
pins her down & breeds her on the ground.
Before she migrates, the female lays her eggs
on the milkweed plant to nourish with its milk.

LXXIV.

In Baddha Konasana, otherwise known as butterfly pose, we sit up straight
& put the soles of our two feet together so that our knees fall outward
like the wings of a butterfly. The Yoga teacher says it is a grounding pose.
*Close your eyes*, she says. *I am, I am,* it is a chant for connection from the
personal self, I am, to the infinite, universal. *I am, I am,* she says. *I am, I
am*, we silently repeat. Our hands folded in prayer. *I am.*

LXXV.

Because vines glue to the tree's
trunk & climb up to the highest coronary,
& like a thick umbilical cord snake down its bark
like a slither in a manifest garden,
until eventually they strangle the life
cell by cell, leaf by leaf, stripping its greenery,
limb by limb, compressing
the cambium's vascular system—
until the trunk, a hollow
totem of itself.
We've watched
the transformation,
from our deck,
season after season,
year after year,
debating whether
to take down one, to protect
the other, the puzzle
of not knowing
which will prosper & which will fail—
& the forever mystery of why, whereas some vines, for instance,
transform over time to birth a healthy sapling,
while others are souls *which quit the case it tore itself from,*
whose seeds cast into the wind & higgledy-piggledy
shoot up for the harpies to feed themselves upon.

LXXVI.

Beneath the soil is an underground system of roots, a connected family that shares their nutrients. If a tree or plant is under duress, sometimes the giving of nutrients from one to the other will bring a sick tree back to life. Further, a tree isolated from other trees is likely to live a shorter life.

LXXVII.

*Truth is destiny,* says
a voice from *Battlefield,*
Peter Brook's version

of *The Mahabharata,*
the epic poem of India
we saw one night at BAM.

War, like every war for power,
destroys a family,
the Kauravas, on one side

are decimated by their cousins
the Pandavas, & the 100 sons of the blind king
strewn across the battlefield.

Everything is inside *The Mahabharata*—
all action controlled by destiny—
& if it isn't there, says the creator, it doesn't exist.

LXXVIII.

In Warrior One, Virabhadrasana, we stand with two feet together,
hands by our sides. We move one leg back & turn our heel into the floor,
the other leg is bent in front, knee above the ankle, our hips turned toward
the center. We raise our hands alongside our ears as if carrying a shield
& breathe. Our teacher says that we are spiritual warriors battling with
self-ignorance, the source of all suffering. *Put yourself at a distance from
the insidious, from the toxic. Observe, be aware of your nature,* she says.
*Breathe.*

LXXIX.

Every year we wrap gilded rhododendron
in a shroud of burlap to withstand weather's

fickle nature (if only we had such a coat)
& once spring arrives strip off its pocked

mask to find reawakened a performance
of dramatic rhododendron. A pink so bright

it is more the red of a beating heart
than the paleness of a fading blush.

But wait, here come the bass, triangle, drums.
The symphony isn't over. One April

we awoke, in storm's aftermath—a brutal,
unbearable, inhabitable night, a mishap

of logic—to find an autopsy of limbs splayed
in the grass, a rotted trunk hurled over,

torn from its roots, where insects
had bed, limbs hurled over grass, corpses

of monarchs curled in humble heads of flowers,
in the lantern carcasses of moths attracted

to light extinguished by dumb suicide.

LXXX.

A drawer of junk jewelry, combs & brushes,
sweatshirts, made-of-honor dress wrapped in cello—

phane & stored like shadows in the closet's
hinterland, diary with crushed pressed

flowers, drawn red hearts, confessions, hopes, dreams,
ink bleeding on onion skin thin as leaves, novels

with pages flagged, postcard of Mexico
I once sent, lock of hair sealed under glass,

of the rashness, impassioned,
forsaken, forever bemused—

a life mask made of strips
of papier-mâché as if to mock

the dead's eternal masquerade.

LXXXI.

*And by came an Angel who had a bright key,*
*And he opened the coffins, and set them all free;*
*Then down a green plain, leaping, laughing, they run*
*And wash in a river, and shine in the sun.*

LXXXII.

Because we did not know,
or failed to know,
were afraid to know,
because we are all fragile,
sisters of survival, daughters
of those who dwell in grief's
bitter smell, descendants who live in fear
of obliteration & unrest, contingent, connected,
roots dug in, twisted, clinging, providing
sustenance & sugar, because in a family,
in our ignorance, pity & pride,
we believed one could not exist
without the other. Because we,
because,
because—

LXXXIII.

The Yoga teacher says we are all unique,
like snowflakes, each its own composition of frozen water,
complex bodies made up of elements necessary for sustaining life:
oxygen, carbon, hydrogen, nitrogen, calcium, phosphorus,
potassium, sulfur, sodium, chlorine & magnesium.
If we focus on our breath, our control shifts from the brain
stem to the cerebral cortex & the mind quiets.
Eyes closed, resting on our backs, out of generosity, kindness,
our teacher sometimes places her two hands beside the back
of our head & elongates the neck to give the body
more room to heal what is broken.

## LXXXIV.

The winter where the sparrows quieted, in which the snow
would not stop, in which the rats would not come out,

in which we feared for our safety & snow covered the bereft shrubs,
homeless (*here I am, I am you*) sought shelter, fearful stockpiled

water & provisions. The winter a strain of virus
quarantined us far into spring, in which another teenager

somewhere in the city is locked in a soporific fog,
helpless, forgotten, isolated in aloneness, landscape

shrouded in an unreasonable mask, winter of the symphony's
grand crescendo—seats of council, judges, assemble to form a decree

citizenry run amok is not a matter of the individual, but society,
timpani, cymbals, snare drum, family of percussion.

LXXXV.

Just like the turning of the clock, ticking away of time,
like the monarch dependent on the milkweed,

milkweed on the monarch, like the faint sound if you listen,
of breathing trees, like a clearing in the forest,

like memory reshaped to form its own inexplicable Horus,
like Demeter holding earth hostage, frozen land its own grave,

until her daughter's freedom from the underworld's
prison of the depraved, like the plot of the myth

concocted to console the inconsolable—
those unwilling to fathom the mind's uncompromising surprise.

LXXXVI.

In 1939 Jews reached the landmark population of seventeen million. After the Holocaust where six million Jews were murdered, the number was reduced to eleven million. Jews make up less than 0.2 percent of the world's population & historically live in fear of extinction.

LXXXVII.

During the blackout, we were alone in our house surrounded by woods
(his father was working in the city). No phone, no access, not even a
radio or batteries for flashlights. Because we wanted him to have faith,
not because we wanted to be separate, but because we had to be watchful
of who we were, we schooled him in the language of our ancestors & so
when darkness descended & he grew afraid, we gathered all the candles. I
told him the story of Moses in the wilderness & how there was a miracle
& the light was everlasting. It is a metaphor, I said & we waited &
eventually we had light.

LXXXVIII.

Paul Celan, a Romanian-Jewish poet growing up in the shadow of the concentration camps, *through the thousand darknesses of death-bringing speech,* drowned himself in the Seine in 1970.

LXXXIX.

flail, snap, struggle,
strangle, some eaten out by an infestation
*(the devastation of dominant manifestation),*
one summer, it was cicadas.
Trunks pregnant with moles & voles,
shelter-seekers making nests—we've spotted swallows,
blue jays, back & forth of robins in idle conversation,
incessant nuisance of woodpeckers—
symphonic throbbing of hundreds of thousands
of insects humming
in brilliant orchestration—watched the nipples
of buds take hold in spring,
shiver in the wind, each leaf, as if to bloom
in spontaneous simulation,
mourned the foliage's decolorization,
curl of leaf before deportation, fallen
leaves, stacked in piles like skeletons
of the dead, under shade & shadow, witnessed
disturbance & succession & as if by the miraculous hand
of a force unknown, tyrannical, victorious, small pines
nearing extinction, through slaughter, no taller
than a toddler, push themselves up & take hold.

## XC.

I don't know if they were weeds or flowers. Or if they were beautiful.
They climbed along the barbed fence in a blaze. The petals were delicate
and translucent. Thorns that pricked & left scratches, if we tried to cut the
blooms for our table. We gave up. They were going to wind the fence
until the sun burned them. Their endurance, like starved bodies after a
winter of war & famine with one purpose in mind, to last until they died.

XCI.

The mind turns inward
after being bound by the actions of the body.
*If there is something you can't let go of, breathe into it,*
the Yoga teacher says. During Savasana, Sanskrit
for corpse or final resting pose, outside, under the tent,
flies buzzing, flat on our backs, arms & legs splayed
open on our mats, as if we're children playing dead,
& she like a victorious warrior on a battlefield, says
to surrender all effort as she walks through the rows.

XCII.

what of those unable to sleep, or dream, or love, or carry a child?

XCIII.

*(thoughts, you torment me)*

XCIV.

Destiny is bigger
than any one of us, says the epic's creator,
individual lives do not matter, valor
will be desecrated & in the battlefield
of time, regardless, like trees,
we all eventually fall.

XCV.

raining, raining, raining, raining,
reigning, reigning, reigning & raining
reigning & raining, raining & raining & raining

XCVI.

By the pool,
we hear them buzzing,
drinking in the honey from our tea,

scent of our suntan lotion. The nest
in the corner of our side table where they breed
seemingly light as a harmless ball of cotton,

a colony of yellow jackets—one
to two thousand waiting—

to anoint the queen.

XCVII.

*The night was dark, no father was there,*
  *The child was wet with dew;*
*The mire was deep, and the child did weep,*
  *And away the vapour flew.*

XCVIII.

*Black milk of daybreak we . . . at night we drink . . . at morning and*
    *midday we*
*. . . at evening, we . . . and we . . .*

XCIX.

Look, here come the cranes, starlings, the dove & then we heard the creak
from a tree, or was it a bird, dark as Hades in the night's malignance,
pecking at the bark. *The miracle is all the days I stayed alive,*
we thought she said.

C.

in which women
are taken from the streets,
refugees sought,
in which children are forced in pens
like pigs & separated from their parents,
in which mothers & fathers grieved
& some went mad from desperation—
one we read took his life—asylum
in which the mind seeks
to keep itself from torture,
asylum where we quarantined
to save humanity,
asylum of thought
& afterthought, asylum
where birds mate & nourish,
asylum in which to seek sanctuary,
rest, asylum we aspire to when we devote
ourselves to a practice, asylum of quiet,
of solitude, of mourning, asylum of love
& gratitude, of words born from chaos
assembled & printed on a page
made from the matter
of a tree, asylum
in which the last generation
of the monarch (or monarchy) lays its eggs
before dying, asylum of—

CI.

Once due to disease we had to cut down a tree to its stump hoping the roots might sprout again around the edges & regenerate. To determine her age, still a baby in terms of the life of trees, we counted the number of circles inside the bark's circumference. Twenty-one rings circled her breadth. Twenty-one years bequeathed to the warmth of the sun, pull from the moon, water from the earth, 7,665 days, 183,960 hours, 11,037,600 minutes in which her long arms locked in the roots & branches of sister trees, shared their sugars, were awash in daylight & if a storm, suffered shaking in brutal darkness.

CII.

In the primal woods (*abandon all hope,*
*you who enter here*) beyond the house,
we hear branches break. More birdcalls.
The incessant swarm of insects, turkeys & pheasants,
vultures searching for prey, a carnival
of breeding. Cries of an orphaned baby fawn
injured, unable to hoist herself up, her mother slaughtered
by stray gunshot dead beside her. One time a school of bats,
like an omen, escaped from the shadow of a tree
& fear startled us to scream
& then we laughed so hard—what else could we do—
we scared the birds. We kept coming back, knowing
the flap of a butterfly wing, for instance, ripple of a storm,
invisible society of connected roots beneath the ground,
(if you break one, you break the other) could change everything.
We trudged until our sneakers were soiled,
until we had sweat through our clothes. Until
like Persephone, in love with herself, greedy, I stopped
to pick some berries from a tree,
& when I looked up, as if put to the test, he was gone.
The trees had become a maze, I lost the path,
a vulture surged overhead as if to claim a body—
yes there were bodies we'd grieved—I thought I saw a creek
opening to a body of water that was dark as the river Styx,
night threatening to descend & before me a fog so thick
it harbored ghosts. Frantic, I wondered if, like her,
I'd lost him forever. *What had I done wrong?*
*Why couldn't I save her?* It wasn't until I followed the last
of the light out of the fog through the clearing
that I saw him, almost ghostlike in the dusk.

CIII.

& relief flooded my fears (*breathe*) & brought me
back to earth.

# NOTES

Two sources were central to the creation of this poetic sequence: *Selected Poems and Prose of Paul Celan*, translated by John Felstiner (Norton, 2001), and *The Inferno of Dante: A New Verse Translation*, by Robert Pinsky (Farrar, Straus & Giroux, 1994).

From Celan:

Epigraph *"Reachable, near and not lost"* and *"Look around"* (Felstiner 395, 77).

[LXXXVIII.] *"through the thousand darknesses of death-bringing speech"* (Felstiner 395).

[XCVIII.] *"Black milk of daybreak we . . . at night we drink . . . at morning and midday we . . . at evening, we . . . and we . . ."* from "Death Fugue" (Felstiner 3).

From Dante:

Dedication, "she who once saw the stars" is from the line "where we come forth, and once more saw the stars."

Epigraphs for all five part titles: *"Love which in gentle hearts is quickly born"* (Pinsky 89), *"Beware how you come in and whom you trust"* (Pinsky 37), *"Now we descend into the sightless zone"* (Pinsky 27), *"If you remove / a little branch"* (Pinsky 129), *"To get back up to the shining world from there"* (Pinsky 373).

[IV.] *"O muses, O geniuses of art, / O memory"* (Pinsky 11).

[XVII.] *"envy, gluttony, & pride igniting their hearts"* (Pinsky 49).

[XXX.] *"hemisphere of darkness"* (Pinsky 29).

[XXXII.] *"made their own house their gallows"* (Pinsky 109, *"made my own house be my gallows"*).

[XLVII.] *"heaven expel him"* (Pinsky 507, *"now heaven expels them"*).

[LXXV.] *"which quit the case it tore itself from"* (Pinsky 105).

[CII.] *"abandon all hope, / you who enter here"* (Pinsky 19).

Other references from published sources:

[XXXI.] *Don't Let Me Be Lonely* refers to the title of Claudia Rankine's poetry volume *Don't Let Me Be Lonely: An American Lyric* (Graywolf Press, 2004).

[V.] *"there is no loneliness like theirs"* is a line from James Wright's poem "A Blessing," which appears in *Above the River: The Complete Poems and Selected Prose* (Wesleyan University Press, 1990).

[XXIX.] "Under microscope, magnifying glass" references the work of Jean-Martin Charcot and the Salpêtrière: www.baillement.com/lettres /Girls_Salpetriere.pdf.

[XXXIII.] *"Suicide isn't an issue"*: This passage comes from a paper written by a student for her AP English class, entitled "Suicide: Effects of a Never Ending Issue," which discussed my book *History of a Suicide: My Sister's Unfinished Life* (Atria, 2011); the paper is also referenced in [XLI.].

[XXXIX.] *"cruellest month"* from *The Waste Land* by T. S. Eliot; *"Tossing their heads"* from "I Wandered Lonely as a Cloud" by William Wordsworth; "too excitable . . . too red," from "Tulips" by Sylvia Plath (*Collected Poems,* Harper & Row, 1981).

[XLV.] *"infants tossed in the air"* is from *Night* by Elie Wiesel (Hill & Wang, 2006).

[LIII.] *"Pretty, pretty robin!"* [LXXXI.] *"And by came an Angel who had a bright key"* [XCVII.] *"The night was dark, no father was there"* from *Songs of Innocence and of Experience* by William Blake.

[LXI.] *"And for your lifeblood I will require a reckoning"* is from Genesis 9:5.

[LXXVII.] *"Truth is destiny"* is from Peter Brook's version of *The Mahabharata*, bam.org/media/7345762; "If it isn't there . . . it doesn't exist . . ." and *"anything it does not contain will be found nowhere"* refer to *Mahabharata: A Modern Retelling* by Carole Satyamurti (Norton, 2015).

Other references and source notes:

[XXXIV.] *"Carbon monoxide is a dangerous gas . . ."* is a direct quote from https://www.cartoq.com/carbon-monoxide-poisoning-death-here-is -how-it-can-happen-in-a-car/.

[XLV.] Swastikas painted on dorm room doors: https://www.insidehighered .com/news/2018/12/05/anti-semitic-incidents-surge-college-campuses -after-pittsburgh-synagogue-shooting; *"Jews will not replace us"*: chant of neo-Nazi marchers in Charlottesville, Virginia, August 12, 2017.

[LXIX.] "we can see the window she peered out" and *"God preserves everything"* are from the emblem at the Gates of the Sheremetev Palace. "Deus conservat omnia," God preserves everything.

[XLVII.] The poem refers to what is now known as the Halloween Massacre, https://www.nytimes.com/2017/10/31/nyregion/police-shooting-lower -manhattan.html.

[XLVIII.] *"What I saw were naked women"* is a direct quote from a news program referencing a Holocaust survivor, and to the Auschwitz Exhibition at the Museum of Jewish Heritage: A Living Memorial to the Holocaust (March 31 evening news, https://mjhnyc.org /auschwitz-exhibition-press/in-the-news/page/4/?filter=auschwitz_press).

[XLIX.] *"I can't breathe"* refers to the chant based on the words of Eric Garner that inspired the Black Lives Matter movement.

[LI.] *"Fire is 1/60 of hell"* from the Talmud, http://www.maqom.com/ passages/050902.pdf.

[XCIII.]: *"thoughts, you torment me"* refers to Aria no. 11 *"Smanie implacabili,"* from Mozart's *Così Fan Tutte*: "Implacable pangs / Which torment me, / Do not subside / Within my being / Until my anguish / Brings me death" (Translation ref 373).

## ACKNOWLEDGMENTS

Grateful acknowledgment is made to the editors of the following publications:

*American Poetry Review:* lii. Pollen is everywhere; liv. Hustling her new book on NPR, a marriage counselor; lv. Snow of childhood; lviii. I don't know if I was still in dream

*Five Points:* xvi. From my window on the third floor; xxiii. Washing dishes, occasionally looking out at the wood; xxvi. We wanted him; xcvi. By the pool

*Gettysburg Review:* xiv. Faith turned on the milkman who delivered; xxxv. Every April a requiem, a re-awakening of dawn, the same chorus; xxxviii. Because her mother was sleeping the sleep of the quiescent; lix. A pigeon flew overhead; lxxix. Every year we wrap gilded rhododendron; lxxxii. Because we did not know; lxxxv. Just like the turning of the clock, ticking away of time

*Granta:* iv. Together we circled; xvii. I knew by then; xxix. Under microscope, magnifying glass; xxx. We kept our heads down; xxxii. Like just awaking; xxxix. Daffodils, survivors, of the *cruellest month;* xlii. like the snap of a branch; xliii. Because it was Christmas & I was home; xlvi. Because gods are threatening to tear down branches; lxi. Metamorphized into trees; lxxx. A drawer of junk jewelry, combs & brushes

*Harvard Review:* i. There she is, the woman who once inhabited; ii. Even the rats will not emerge in the whiteout—; viii. We can't see anything but ice

*Orion:* vii. Each season with its privileges

*Prairie Schooner:* xxii. Those long afternoons we trudged; xli. The boy who arrived; xliv. Turquoise plates extremely rare, as the orange footed

*Provincetown Arts Magazine:* vi. After the wind tore up; xxiv. & so we looked for patterns . . . ; xxv. Trees breathe in oxygen . . . ; xxvii. Pollen, like sperm to humans; xxviii. In tree pose, otherwise known as Vriksasana . . . ; lvi. In Yoga class the teacher says; lxxii. The monarchs are born. They are smaller this year; lxxiii. Butterflies sometimes mate as soon as the male emerges; lxxiv. In Baddha Konasana, otherwise known as butterfly pose, we sit up straight; lxxvi. Beneath the soil is an underground system of roots . . . ; lxxvii. *Truth is destiny,* says; lxxviii. In Warrior One, Virabhadrasana . . . ; xci. The mind turns inward; xciv. Destiny is bigger; xcv. raining, raining, raining, raining; ci. Once due to disease; ciii. & relief flooded my fears (*breathe*) & brought me

*Virginia Quarterly Review:* ix. & in the mornings sometimes awoke so cold; xi. In Iowa City, the restaurant; xii. Why I thought I needed to rent a third-floor attic; xviii. Like a flock of dispossessed; xx. If someone was kind enough . . . ; xl. When he was small; l. What are words when they meet the action; lxviii. I was washing dishes in the sink

xcvi. By the pool will appear in *Buzz Words: Poems about Insects,* Everyman's Library Pocket Poets, Alfred A. Knopf

I am indebted to Sarah Chalfant and Jacqueline Ko at the Wylie Agency; at Alfred A. Knopf to John Gall for this beautiful cover, Todd Portnowitz, and my editor, Deborah Garrison, for her brilliant instincts; Eavan Boland, John Kinsella, Forrest Gander; David Baker for generous readings; Dana Montlack for the gorgeous frontispiece; to my family for everything.

## A NOTE ABOUT THE AUTHOR

Jill Bialosky is the author of four acclaimed collections of poetry, most recently *The Players;* three critically acclaimed novels, most recently *The Prize;* a *New York Times* best-selling memoir, *History of a Suicide: My Sister's Unfinished Life;* and *Poetry Will Save Your Life: A Memoir.* Her poems and essays have appeared in *Best American Poetry, The New Yorker, The Atlantic, Harper's Magazine, O, the Oprah Magazine, The Kenyon Review, Harvard Review,* and *The Paris Review,* among others. She coedited, with Helen Schulman, the anthology *Wanting a Child.* She is executive editor and vice president at W. W. Norton & Company. Her work has been a finalist for the James Laughlin Prize, the Patterson Prize, and Books for a Better Life. In 2014, she was honored by the Poetry Society of America for her distinguished contribution to poetry. She lives in New York City.

*A Note on the Type*

The text of this book was set in Sabon, a typeface
designed by Jan Tschichold (1902–1974).

*Designed and typeset by Michael Collica*

*Printed and bound by Friesens,*
*Altona, Manitoba*